SANCTUARY

SANCTUARY

SHAYLA HERRÓN

NEW DEGREE PRESS
COPYRIGHT © 2021 SHAYLA HERRÓN
All rights reserved.

SANCTUARY

ISBN   978-1-63730-437-2 *Paperback*
           978-1-63730-531-7 *Kindle Ebook*
           978-1-63730-532-4 *Ebook*

This book is dedicated to every soul that reads it.

CONTENTS

AUTHOR'S NOTE	13
AT THE ALTAR	**19**
WHEN I LEARNED ABOUT GENDER	20
HER LOCKDOWN	22
A PREDATOR ON THE MARCH	23
SELL ME	24
WHY ME?	25
WHY ME, AGAIN ...	27
FAMILY	29
RUINS	30
LIKE A LOTUS	**33**
NAKED IN WINTER	34
INTERCOURSE IS	35
RAINY DAY BLUES	37
THE BEST FIG OF HIS LIFE	39
LOVE IS ...	**41**
GRAND RISING	42

AS YOUR BLACK WOMAN, I LOVE YOU HARDER EACH DAY	44
SOMETHING REAL	45
SOUL MATE	47
PARADISE	48
SELFLOVE	49
SORRY WILL NEVER BE ENOUGH	50
THE WORST KIND OF FAILURE	51
LOVE LANGUAGES	52
LETTING GO?	**55**
MY INQUISITION	56
TRIFLES WON'T SAVE US	58
"ARE WE CLOSE ENOUGH?"	60
ONE NIGHT STAND	61
RARE BLOOMING	62
ABORTION	63
ONE OF THE HARDEST PEOPLE TO LOVE	64
UN(DE)R (PRESS)URE	**67**
DISPENSABLE	68
2:45 A.M.	69
WILL I?	72
NUMBING THE PAIN	74
GRIEF	75
FALSE MEMORIES	78
WHEN I KNEW I WANTED TO LIVE	80
POINT OF VIEW	**83**
WAR AND PEACE	84
WHEN I GO TO D.C.	85
BLACK AUTUMN	88
STOP!	89

TAKING TIME	91
BREAKS	93
THE HE/ART	94
LES BI ANEST	97
BLACK CHURCHES	99
OCEAN AND STARS	100
RELIGION REMASTERED	**103**
EVERY SUNDAY	104
OPEN MY HEART, LORD	105
IT WAS YOU	107
TO HEAR FROM GOD	110
TO MY ABBA FATHER	111
THE PURGE	**113**
SO ANXIOUS	114
SO, YOU HAVE PTSD …	115
EVER IN MY HEART	116
CONVERSATION WITH MY THERAPIST	117
MY FATHER IN OTHER MEN	119
HER ONLY SUPPORTER	121
WHEN I CAN'T LOVE MYSELF ENOUGH	124
PULSE	125
METAMORPHOSIS	126
MOON PHASES	128
SOUL SAVER	129
THE F WORD	**131**
MY KOBE	132
HOW TO MOVE ON WHEN THEY CUT YOUR LEGS	133
FORGIVING ME	134

THE BENEDICTION	**137**
THE ENSLAVED AND THE MASTER	138
FROM MY FLESH TO MY SPIRIT	140
IF I COULD CHANGE ANYTHING, IT WOULD BE ME ...	141
LEMONS TO LEMONADE, LEMON CAKE, LEMON PIE	142
VIRGO	143
SANCTUARY	145
ACKNOWLEDGEMENTS	149

"As my sufferings mounted I soon realized that there were two ways in which I could respond to my situation—either to react with bitterness or seek to transform the suffering into a creative force. I decided to follow the latter course."

—DR. MARTIN LUTHER KING JR.

AUTHOR'S NOTE

―

Dear Readers,

If seventeen-year-old Shayla knew that all the pain she experienced would produce such a transcending work of art that would later heal people, she would have fought even harder to save her life. Nonetheless, she fought hard enough ...

Initially I struggled with what I wanted this book to be about. I jumbled back and forth between a few creative ideas. But I lost enthusiasm for those ideas. I did not want this book to be about my skills as a poet. I did not want this to be an act of showboating and seeing how many images and words I could shove into a piece. I wanted to be as authentic as possible. I wanted the readers of this book to do more than read—I want you to experience every piece as if you are lying on a beach with only the sunset, the peace of roaring waters, and squawking gulls as a distraction. This book needed simplicity.

So, I decided to write about something personal. *Sanctuary* is filled with my tears, trauma, and the essence that helped me to evolve, heal, and see the world as it is and not as an obstruction. This is my first book—an introduction to who I am as a person and as a growing writer.

Some of the intersections and themes in this book include trauma and expression, religion and resentment, and loss and healing. There are various forms of pieces, including blank verse, rhymed, free verse, narrative, elegies, and many more. As a writer, some of my inspirations are Nikki Giovanni, Toni Morrison—may she rest in peace—bell hooks, Ms. Maya Angelou—may she rest in peace—Ntozake Shange, and Frances E. W. Harper—may she rest in peace. These writers emulate the freedom in writing I desire to have as a Black woman.

One of the major underlying themes I explored and taught myself in the writing of this book is the intersectionality between trauma and writing. I formed a timeline of when I began to write. The first time someone recognized I could make something out of what I write was my fifth-grade homeroom teacher, Ms. Wheeler. She felt a need to tell my parents how well written my work was. Little does Ms. Wheeler know—from that moment on—my parents instilled her observations in me, and I began to write every day. I was ten years old exploring all I could with words, writing about love and the beauty in the world around me.

At the age of eleven I began puberty. Life at home took a turn for the worst—which I touch on in this book—and I was sexually assaulted. After this moment, the healthy thirst I once had for writing began to dry out. I was eleven and I wanted to end my life. I had never seen or heard of suicide before this. My suicidal thoughts were organic and influenced every decision I would later make in life. It is safe to assume that was all I wrote about, which did not help. It fed the darkness.

I battled with suicidal ideation for almost ten years. I experienced more traumatic events outside of the home. After age eleven I was sexually assaulted three more times. My relationship with my body was connected through hatred. If I hated my body, I hated everything else about myself. Every poem I wrote—until my junior year of college—was about pain and trauma. My growth and skills as a writer were stagnated.

I later learned—from my professor at Bowie State University—that when you experience trauma one of your five senses is inhibited, making it difficult to recall all of what was felt in the moment it happened. I also found that most of us can still be triggered by it—depending on which one of our senses was most heightened at the moment of trauma. I went to therapy to deal with this.

My therapist—who is my therapist to this day—helped me cultivate who I am through healing and learning, leading me to want to get a degree in counseling myself. Most sessions she would let me talk until my mind went blank. Then she would ask me a question that helped unlock good memories I had forgotten I had. I want to help people heal. A friend once told me that my words and actions saved his life—during a time where I was dealing with my own depression. For him to say that was unbelievable. I realized I had a purpose to heal people.

Every therapist seems to believe that words heal people. In my case, however, the words I produced only fed the darkness and pain. My state of mind needed to be changed. I needed to heal beyond words. I do believe words heal people, but poets have a keen sense of the difference between communicating and expressing. I had to get to a place of communicating in a way where my words would be felt, understood, and known. Expression is what gets people in trouble and leaves them misunderstood by family and peers. Expression cannot be felt by everyone. When you communicate, the masses will understand. For example, Dr. Martin Luther King Jr.'s "I Have a Dream" speech communicates injustice and presents unity as a solution, while also allowing King's personal feelings to be felt. Poetry has not healed me, but poetry has helped me see how much I have evolved.

Beyond therapy, I started going to church and reading the Bible, which helped me to learn more about spirituality. The stories in the Bible helped to heal and empower me as a woman. They communicated with me. There is a story in the Gospels about a woman with the "issue of blood." This woman bled for twelve years and was condemned by the people in her town. She heard of the miracles that Yeshua, Joshua, or Jesus the Christ, had performed. This woman had faith that Jesus could end her torment. As he was passing through her town she touched his garment—and was healed. Her faith and strength saved her life. The strength I had saved mine as well.

Religion and Spirituality are the reason why this book is entitled *Sanctuary*. I learned that in a sanctuary you talk to God, you heal, and you weep. A sanctuary is a free space, and this book is just that. It is a free space where the tears that dripped from eyes molded into words.

I pursued a degree in creative writing before I realized that I wanted to pursue counseling. I wanted writing to be something filled with life, as it had been before the trauma. I did not want it to be a coping mechanism.

As aforementioned, I met a professor at my university and took several of his courses. His teachings influenced the writer that I am today, cultivating my skills and bringing back my healthy thirst for writing. My growth and skills were no longer stagnant, and I could communicate. In his course I developed over 500 images—encompassing alliteration, metaphors, and other literary devices—that were all, surprisingly, not about pain.

I want to show readers that we have to go back to the moments that have hurt us and ask how they have shaped us. I want whoever reads this to apologize to themselves and the ones who hurt them, allowing ourselves to heal and reflect. This book is for anyone who has ever felt lost. It is for those of us who need to reflect on and revisit our trauma. It is for college students, young adults, and maybe even teens. It is for the poet that lives inside of us all. This book is also interactive to encourage reflection. At the end of section, there is a page entitled "For Your Use" for the reader to write their thoughts on each section— whether it be anything you would like to remember—how it made you feel, etc. Please feel free to contact me if the time comes when you would like to share your thoughts.

I will warn you that some of these pieces are very realistic and may trigger you. I extend caution before moving forward. Nonetheless, this book also prompts reflection on what we have all overcome at some point in our lives. It will make you stop and look at the life around you. *Sanctuary* reminds us to check on people and ourselves consistently. This book will make you want to take care of yourself.

It is time for us all to be able to communicate, to feel, to think, and to understand.

AT THE ALTAR

When I Learned about Gender

We were both three,
too young to be confined
by rules of Christianity,
saying Hell is the only place
for men who lay with men
Homophobes who spit at you
while on a date with the man
you love, and misplaced Masculinity,
whose purpose was to only play god
We were gender free, or so we believed

I asked you, which color?
You told me pink,
because it was bright
And you wanted everyone
to see, and say, "how pretty!"
We were gender free
I painted your nails
with dry stains hanging
off the side, I never painted
in the lines, but that was how
you liked it, messy, because
we were three
We were gender free

Different parts,
beyond that I believed
us to be the same
Boy and Girl weren't words
that needed rules

We would play
as children should,
we were gender free,
we were happy

Before, we could let
everyone see, and be happy too,
about what we believed was art—
and no one can deny art,
especially the design of a child
whose heart only
aims to please—
unexpectedly, your father slapped you
to the ground, you looked
up, he asked,
"Are you a faggot?"
You couldn't speak,
as he kicked into your premature ribs,
did you live past this moment?

You and I, as polish is taken
off of you, confused,
thinking, "What does gay mean?"
I cried because you cried
We were gender free
until that moment, when
I learned that Boy and Girl
aren't just words,
it's a lifestyle, or maybe
a prison, whatever way
you see it, we were not happy
we were not gender free.

Her Lockdown

Eyes compressed,
crusty crumbs building up,
bringing out images of tranquility
riding on clouds with LoveALot,
Tenderheart, Cheer, Funshine,
Wish. To never wipe the crust,
only knowing time after dusk
and never dawn. Things go wrong.

Eyes wiped, not by the hands
one was born with, but of another
ripped clothes, black and blue bruises,
sweating over the stained white
stove, sliding to grip waist,
quivers, drops, bacon grease on the
chest. Burning flesh is not breakfast.

Eyes bleeding, unhealed cuts reopened
from yesterday, unwanted thumb pressing into
lower limbs. Sacred no more, belonging
to only the man born of, you close your
eyes, there is the clouds and LoveALot,
TenderHeart, Cheer, Funshine,
Wish. To stay in fantasy,
as his grunts become nothing,
no longer triggering.

a predator on the march

depressed timberland
a heavy, keen hammer prowling
at the virgin girl.

Sell Me

His hooves penetrated
deep in my neck,
leaving a brand
like a slave in the "New World"
being sold at an auction.

Why Me?

My body aches from all the men that touched me
without asking.
Bacteria from hands, saliva from mouths,
unwanted transfers of DNA from penes still
sit on my beautiful brown skin—
I tried to wash it away,
multiple showers a day,
multiple prayers to God,
multiple distractions—men and women alike—
who used my time just to waste it.
Questioning my worth—
costing the same as porcelain plates in a Dollar Tree,
everyone knows someone who has shopped or stole from a
Dollar Tree,
because everything is close to free and won't be missed.
This is how I feel, free to anyone and not myself, Dollar
Tree.
Why me?

Ignorant men and women will say,
"she asked for it … ,"
"it's always the quiet ones … ," or maybe,
"it's always the one with a bad attitude … ,"
but to the hateful and predatory
it don't matter the body type,
as long as there is "ass and titties" as the rappers say—
any aperture, channel, furrow, or opening—
there's no acts of discrimination in rape,
and like Dollar Tree, no acts of discrimination

in what gets bought or stolen from each aisle.
If they want it, they get it.

Becoming obsessed with being pure,
convincing others of my purity but never myself,
covering up, hiding my curves and my hurt, screaming,
"God is good!" and "Praise the Lord!" in church.
Outside of "holy grounds", still feeling like a Dollar Tree
I moved past my panic of being overly shopped at,
letting them all shop freely,
violating me more than before.

Why Me, Again ...

Now the man I love touches me,
it feels the same as men I didn't love.
The first man's face and name I can't remember,
only the sensation of where he touched me remains.
The second and third were men I trusted, calling them friends,
never accepting rides from anyone again.
The fourth was a stranger who snuck into my hotel room
on vacation.
Someone I thought I'd never see again, until I saw him
on TV,
in the middle of a play with his college football team.
The last, causing the most discomfort,
was the love of my teenage years.

Today someone made me question myself.
Helping others as a distraction from my traumas,
something so complicated—you get over it—or so it seems.
When I find myself unoccupied,
their voices creep up on me again.
Breathing in my ear, forcibly moving in and out,
"whose pussy is this?"
and again, and again.
To be free of people who own part of your soul,
the end of lifelong feats at the outerends of my valley,
a place I may never reach—
I'm still walking.

I apologize to the men I forced to love me.
The men I forced to comfort me.

Making myself uneasy to love,
I am no better than my abusers.
I used you all, like they used me.
I used you until you weren't enough.
Sometimes my body and mind don't agree,
one desires to be pleased,
the other wants to run.

Can I ever love unconditionally?
Will I get over this?
Stop overdosing in front of my family—

I cannot disappoint.

I slowly drift into the shadow of my past,
lifting the burden of myself.

I circle back,
Can I be pure again?

Family

Oftentimes, I saw no harm in it.
Imagine being six, receiving arousal as a gift
instead of the pink bike I wanted.
Ten years later saying, "I don't like hugs, sorry,
I'm claustrophobic,"
claim to be introverted,
clinging to the web
out of curiosity and comfort,
knowing it's killing me

I'll be in and out of hospitals,
sneaking out,
high off marijuana laced with purple crystals,
cutting into the blue rivers on my wrists,
washing my hazel skin red

Pregnant by a married man twice my age,
I can't keep it so I'll be,
laid back with a bright lamp in my face
and a nurse saying,
"one big breath in for me."

I'll force other people to please me,
not caring if they're ready,
being the reason why they have trust issues,
can't look at themselves in the mirror
or see themselves, without the trauma,
a pure soul longing to smell the roses.

Ruins

When my sacred grounds
become ruins too soon—
a place for none to enter—
Anyone who dares
will face the wrath of my trauma
because I don't want to be rebuilt,
just left to wallow in self-sorrow.

FOR YOUR USE

Take a moment to reflect on the section you have just read.

Maybe something I wrote resonated with you and raised a question, or helped you recall a memory.

What abuse have you been subject to?

This question is not exact. It is only to help generate thought.

Write your response down here.

LIKE A LOTUS

Naked in Winter

Noses touch, breathing at the same pace,
heating this room—windows are cracked—the crisp winter air seeps in.
Lips glide against each other, only to feel skin and not kiss,
our legs intertwined with no rush to penetration,
hands, rubbing my back, engulfing it,
wrapping around my neck like a scarf.
Warmth rising from our nether regions—
we're on a beach in the Caribbean.
Chest to chest, eye to eye, palm to palm,
the only sound, the crashing of our waves,
translating to say *I love you*, with every part of me.
Arousing ourselves, teaching intimacy,
so close, feeling flesh that melts to become one.

INTERCOURSE IS

INTERCOURSE IS LIBERATION,
REALIZATION OF PHYSICAL BEAUTY.
RELIGION TAUGHT ME IT A SIN
WHEN IT'S NOT—
IT'S NATURE RUNNING ITS COURSE
THROUGH MAN, WOMAN, CREATING SHAPES,
BENDING WAISTS, SWEAT, FIFTY-EIGHT FACETS,
BROWN BODIES SWIMMING SIMULTANEOUSLY,
WEAVING TO CONNECT CURVES. IT'S
RELEASING CHEMICALS, RELIEVING STRESS,
PROCLAIMING LOVE, CREATING LIFE—
INTERCOURSE IS LIBERATION.
IT'S MORE THAN AN INWARD AND OUTWARD
MOTION
TO FREEDOM, THE INCANTATION
THAT REPEATS IN THE MIND,
MOUNTED UP ON A STALLION,
GRINDING AGAINST GRAVITY,
RIDING TO THE TOP OF THE HILL,
WHITE FLAG IN HAND, WAITING TO RELEASE.
IT'S THE ONLY WAR WHERE BOTH SIDES WIN.
NO NEED FOR COMPROMISE, WEARING OUT
INSIDES.
EVERY BEING WANTS IT—NO—
NEEDS IT, AND THEY NEED IT RIGHT, MAKING
ONE COME BACK FOR MORE AND MORE.
INTERCOURSE IS LIBERATION.
IT'S THE PUREST DRUG. WHEN FELT,
HUGGING NOT ONLY THE BODY BUT THE SOUL.
IT CAN HEAL THE HATE OF TOUCH

WHEN THE RIGHT ONE OPENS YOU UP
WHEN THERE IS NOTHING TO FEAR,
WHEN THEY TAKE CARE OF THE BODY
YOU SHARE,
INTERCOURSE IS LIBERATION.
INTERCOURSE IS A REVELATION,
EVOLVING EVERY ROUND LIKE A REVOLUTION.

Rainy Day Blues

I can remember the day you were conceived.
Your father waking me up with his tongue
Battle of the Sexes, grasp of this lock and key.
I can hear the blues playing in the background
through my black and blue speaker,
in the far-left corner of the bed.
Heavy rain pour complementing
our sounds of putty,
your father, sweating profusely,
droplets beginning from his hairline
falling to my breasts,
I, dripping wet,
making my own café au lait.

Reaching to the climax of this blues song,
going on forever, on a loop,
I manipulate it, like a charmer to a
serpent, seducing its prey, and
he knew it too, by the look in my eyes.
He climbed up and inside my mahogany
bay to the perfect spot, making him shake—
thirty seconds pass and it's over—
The blues song has stopped.

The caesura I did not see.
Now I'm here in April, sitting up
against my five-foot headboard,
waiting for the day I get to see you,
and November is not far.
Your father and I have forgotten each other,

his face you'll never see,
but I believe in irony,
I'm sure I'll see his face in you.

the best fig of his life

taste buds
commemorate this fig,
brown outer layer,
perspirations,
pink, purple, red insides.
saliva drips
after each bite,
this fig, the highlight
of his life.
digging so deep,
eating white seeds
when he shouldn't.
now it's vacant.

FOR YOUR USE

Take a moment to reflect on the section you have just read.

What things in your life have liberated you?
Have you ever struggled with body image? What helped you overcome this struggle?

These questions are not exact. They are only to help generate thought.

Write your responses down here.

LOVE IS ...

Grand Rising

the smell of lint covers my house,
its flurries coming from Rah on a
mild spring morning, the ones seen
between shades in the spotlight
that lands on the bedroom floor,
the window is cracked,
winds blowing wooden blinds
scraping the sides of the windowblock
to the right of the bed.
my body jumps like waking up
with sweats from a bad dream,
swinging one leg after the other
from under the covers, standing up,
and after I have reached for miles—
northeast, southwest, and a quarter behind me—
by chance, my curiosity lends me
to gaze out of the window,
as I pull my waistlength box braids
out of my bonnet and up into a ponytail,
wiping the crust from my eyes,
picking up my glasses,
case-less on the oakwood dresser,
pushing them on crookedly—
left temple poking my outer
ear—without cleaning them, it's smudged,
but there he is, the love of my life,
blasting Tupac from his car,
kicking around the gravel

in my Carolina driveway,
making each rise better
than all of my falls.

As Your Black Woman, I Love You Harder Each Day

Because one day you may leave me—
not out of desire—but because you'll forget
to put on your turning signal at an intersection,
getting pulled over, and as you prepare your license and registration,
the one sworn to protect you will see you reaching over,
enabling his disposition, ridding of you before you look back,
and see the eyes of the man who takes your life.

Something Real

I see the enthusiasm in your eyes
as if this is your first time experiencing love.
I've known many men,
who you never cared to know,
loving me like you're my first,
erasing all past hurt.

You've known only one woman,
yet it does not show.
Everything about you feels fresh,
like reaching out my hand
under the sprinklers at a supermarket,
as water hits it and the vegetables underneath.

I feel the enthusiasm in your touch,
when you slide your hand
up my back to hold my head,
gazing at me like a cub to its mother,
as if this is your first time seeing new life.

Even in times when I get frustrated,
saying "you don't do enough",
when you haven't been taught
beyond the bare minimum,
I'll share it and be patient.

I must show you the world,
planning all of our dates and trips,
teaching you how to massage a woman's body,
why music always makes intercourse better.

I must show you why spontaneity keeps love alive,
telling you to get dressed without warning,
driving an hour out to another state,
dancing on a boat playing Drake.

To you, effort is just showing up,
that's okay for now,
because I know one day you'll give me the world
back, everything tangible I always wanted.
seeing each day the more you sacrifice,
seeing each day the individual you are,
seeing that this is something real,
the more I heal …

Soul Mate

I remember when it was you and I,
fighting off my anxiety.

You took me back to my past,
a place where I was always afraid to go.

You made me bound to being set free.

Where all my demons lurked, now angels hover.

At midnight, my thoughts would take over—
You saved me.

You're the fire beneath my earth,
Your passion flows through my soul.

Your waters nurture my dry heart.

You make me feel safe, I am not afraid of
anything, as long as I live life next to you.

paradise

is living on an island with you,
going to the market on a Saturday,
picking the same sea bass and cod,
cooking the same chowder and stew,
driving to the same cave with fireflies,
laying bare for hours as we prepare,
to do this all again the next day.

SelfLove

I was told that when they say I love you,

and you don't feel the same,

never say it back

for the sake of saving face.

When they no longer please you,

when they no longer show effort—

no more flowers at your door,

compliments to fill a gallon jar,

kisses on the forehead and cheek,

or, "hey baby I have a surprise—"

Look them in the eyes,

say that your core

no longer flutters at the sight of them,

nor at the sound of their voice.

I was told to never feel guilt

when I choose myself.

Sorry Will Never Be Enough

I am sorry I cheated all those years ago—
I never properly apologized,
or told the truth.
I continued to lie and
couldn't see the pain it caused.
Until today. I woke up—
I had dreamt about you,
devaluing yourself,
when you were always beautiful,
inside and out,
you were giving me you
despite your scars—
My insecurities,
drowning out the love,
which others couldn't see, but
I really did love you.
Do I love you now?—
Yes.
I do not believe people move on from relationships—
It's an act of repressing emotions.
I never met someone who I once loved,
and stopped loving.
I found someone to love harder—
who loved me harder.
Even if we speak on hatred,
that grew from love,
once you stop hating them,
it will always go back to love.

The Worst Kind of Failure

"I've never been in love,"

A lie I breathe in daily like oxygen,
escaping the hurt that comes
with failed relationships.

"I don't know how to love,"

A lie to keep myself
from committing
to the right one.

"I keep attracting the same types,"

Always wanna fight,
overwhelmed by my brevity
in confrontation,

I become the jester,
believing I need,
fixing.

Love Languages

Lacking physical affections as an adolescent—
forehead kisses, hugs when I came home from school,
cuddles when I was sick—
Given a spoonful of neglect,
and had to bear its foul taste alone.
Excuses of, "You're older now,"
and these figurative drawls I never put on
Birthed as separation anxiety,
got a partner who feels like a sex worker,
on call whenever I need it.
Quality time on a scale,
wavering violently
between codependency and manipulation,
losing individuality,
dragging them down with me.
I was showered with gifts,
dangling price tags
don't impress me.
I think I would prefer acts of service, but—
I have never been with someone
who has offered me the chance to experience it.

FOR YOUR USE

Take a moment to reflect on the section you have just read.

What is love to you?
How has loved healed some of your trauma?
What have you not realized about love until now?
Does real love truly hurt?
Can people choose who they fall in love with?

These questions are not exact. They are only to help generate thought.

Write your responses down here.

LETTING GO?

My Inquisition

Every time he speaks,
I am being manipulated.
What is the truth?
I told him,
forgiveness is hard,
but he keeps hurting me.
Is this how a relationship
is supposed to feel?
Constant arguing,
until you reach
a point of bliss?
What happens,
when the honeymoon phase ends?
Are you no longer
good for each other,
are you supposed
to figure it out?
Growing up,
I never had a depiction
of a good marriage.
One parent—
constantly cheating,
on the one,
they claimed to love—
and the other,
constantly screaming,
"you're lying!"
so, I always think
he's lying.
Are there supposed

to be phases of unhappiness?
Am I supposed to feel
disgusted when I look
at him?
Is it disgust,
or am I afraid?
When we argue,
he gaslights me.
It makes me,
believe him less.
It makes me,
think less of myself.
I feel like he's lying.
I feel like he's lying.
I think,
he's lying.

What am I doing,
What am I doing to myself,
What am I doing?

trifles won't save us

the spirits tell me it won't work
got a silver wrist band,
its cursive inscription,
"forever"
devoted to myself,
but these voices
coming from people
i cannot see—
mock me,
mock my love,
our love, whispering,
"your love for each other
won't keep you"
"is your love even real?,"
"not on the same page anymore,"
"leave him,"
"forget him,"
i scream,
pacing my room,
banging my head on a wall

to fight harder
i got a gold necklace
with your initial on it
making my love stronger,
placing it in objects
no one can take from me
you left me,
the necklace turned bronze,
the voices have stopped

i've come to accept,
these spirits were right,
trifles can't save love
which didn't exist.

"are we close enough?"

sex won't resolve
we haven't learned
bicker
confusion thicker

call me a bitch
spit on my face
slap me to the floor
mad at yourself
in love with a whore

our daughter will see
you will tell her,
"get a towel"
for my eye
that you busted open,
as the cream carpets
become cherry wine

are we close enough?
is this the vow
i made till i die?

One Night Stand

Waking up and you're not there,
the call has ended.
Falling asleep on the phone
is for both people to still be there,
to say good morning or grand rising.
You've hung up to take your walk of shame
into the kitchen, where you pull out
week old box of Cheerios and open
the fridge, to find you have no milk.

Rare Blooming

Look at us, promised we'd cultivate like the Juliet rose,
look at us, in the spring season, and nothing shows.

You promised me a love rare as the Middlemist Red,
when tears of torment are the only thing I shed.

You said you would take me out each year for
our anniversary,
feeling like the one night when the Nightblooming
Cereus appears.

I wanted to see the Hibiscus immaculatus,
but you'd rather betray my trust, falling victim to lust,

yearning for a quick bust, over a Jade Vine,
exotic, and ever absorbing your time.

You thought our love extinct like the Gibraltar Campion,
but it was still here, hanging on through this last feat.

Again, these women call to you like the Parrot's Beak.
Seeing no place for me in your heart,

I let you go, rendering myself weak.
Dying and reincarnating as the Corpse Flower,
waiting years to see another man flock to my peak.

Abortion

From choosing life
to believing in choice

Questioning another's decision
then making the same one

One day, I was pregnant
the next day, I was not

I would ask you to promise
not to judge me
but that fear only
comes from the remnants
of my predisposition

I understand free will
in the way God saw fit
living life to experience
not to perfect it

one of the hardest people to love

dating a man
from the hood
is never easy
they will love you
from a distance
only need you
when they get angry
you'll calm them down
relax their thoughts
when they relive their trauma
from seeing a girl
get her innocence stolen
from being acquaintances with meth
birthing an addiction
from their mother's death
to being homeless
building cardboard castles

to realizing they can never love
you properly
because they know pain
more

FOR YOUR USE

Take a moment to reflect on the section you have just read.

What heartbreaks are you not allowing yourself to feel?
What are you having trouble letting go of?
What has your journey with personal relationships been like?

These questions are not exact. They are only to help generate thought.

Write your responses down here.

UN(DE)R (PRESS)URE

dispensable

3 a.m.
drive
two suicidal people
at the beach
waves
attraction
swimming out
serenity
waves
catch him
silence

        achieving what i could not.

2:45 A.M.

I can't seem to stop
the tears from falling,
I can't seem to catch a thought
because they're racin'.
Pain in my chest,
I'm too complacent.
Trynna figure out
where this all began,
I ran,
now I can barely stand,
because I'm still running,
I'm half dead,
don't know what
I'm running from,
but I know it's a burden,
a burden carrying a burden,
that's what I'm worth,
nothing.
Visions of foaming
out the mouth,
the only thing
holding me up
was my father's hands,
siblings
in the kitchen,
paramedics rushing in,
only God knows
how they view me,
I say,
"screw me,"

cause I know,
this screwed them.
No love, no energy,
could set me free—
no money, no degree,
can drop this heat.
My life is on fire,
and I'm waitin' for the choir,
casket breaking my back,
because I was birthed with it.
No judgment,
is what I want to acquire,
but I'm living
to be judged
on that great day,
I think I'm being played.
Don't like to be disappointed,
but I always disappoint,
I'm tired,
my parents ask me how,
always missing the points.
My joints crack,
then they'll break,
and for what,
whose who,
too-many's,
risk did I take?
I lie awake,
till six (6,6)
cookies bake,
they burn,
lay sideways,

holding to a crucifix.
The beast,
just trynna get in my mind
it's deep,
hard to find balance,
no serenity, no peace,
a catastrophe,
plus tax and fees.
Can't be like my uncle,
grandma saying,
"you sound like him,",
heard his demons got in,
but he did win,
he's somewhere better
than here,
where your fears are alive,
your ears and eyes bleed
from the evil you hear and see,
I can't breathe,
no George Floyd,
but I'm Floyd,
and it's never may,
I can't weather these storms,
I'm torn ......

Will I?

Fall victim
to my triggers,
thigh grip,
waist hugs,
whispers in my ears,
"you like that?"
thinking I would rather die.

Conversations
about battered mothers,
imagining myself
with black eyes,
garnet bruises,
and for the sake
of my loneliness,
letting a man
my children don't know,
drag their pubescent skin
across the carpet,
burning for eternity.

Hearing
the word, "but,"
knowing
rejection follows.
For the sake of survival,
forgetting my morals,
selling my body
a few blocks from

my grandmother's church,
in hopes that someone
might save me.

numbing the pain

for years i used to ask myself,
"why do people cut their skin?"

now i understand why,
it's about numbing the pain,

when it becomes unbearable,
or maybe it's because—

they've grown numb,
and long to feel again.

Grief

A stony world,
was the day when
my greatgrandmother
was taken from me.
Midnight exactly,
she was taken from me.
Overcome by shock,
I had not noticed
the mirror ball dropping.
Denial consumed me,
shortly after
reality was gripping.

Rage—,
blistering like bare feet
against summer concrete—,
fueled me, which God received
in immensity.
The all-knowing, most high,
has stolen from me.
He, who has need of nothing,
performed not a miracle,
but a monstrosity.
Questions in my mind
being blown around rapidly,
I could not catch one
to set me free.

Lost in a labyrinth
constructed by agony,

I bargained with God.
If He permitted
her breath and mobility,
fidelity—
the covenant I would keep.
He presented me
with three promises,
I was eleven and naïve,
choosing one blindly,
none giving my nanny
extended longevity.

Depression,
always wanting to carpool
my hair became a bird's nest,
an insomniac, I could not rest,
a full moon cycle later, a pool
of memories taking over my mind,
prohibiting more
of what I longed for,
rest.

What did I miss?
The trail of smoke
beginning in the kitchen,
making its way
to my room as pumpkin pie.
Her stories of nonfiction fiction,
making it easier than to lie.
Now in a fog of desolation,
it's mist made of tears I cried,

with no religion,
death was the only vision.

I kept Acceptance on hold
for nine years.
Enabled to answer its call,
awakened after all the tears
who decided
to surrender its fall,
God's creation needed me,
its inhabitants
needed this narrative.
I know now,
while we are apart,
her sharp words I honor,
no matter my evolvement.

False Memories

Living with you,
was like living with dust
clinging to banisters.
Dust of my life,
you abandoned us,
feeling inclined
to come back,
I was elated at the time,
until only pain,
followed.

Mother's tears—
the dawn of my cold heart,
emerging myself in drugs,
developing addictive tendencies,
many men,
who stroked my ego,
just for a stroke back,
opening up
my heart to voodoo,
bewitching
all who fell to me,
running naked
from random apartments,
caught stealing
more than their hearts,
erratic and unstable,
my breathing,

my love life,
some sins I'd never tell,
but I hide them in this knife.

When I Knew I Wanted to Live

The father I proclaimed to hate
grappled my body,
holding my life with me,
calmly repeating my name,
asking me questions like,
How many did you take?
He treated me as all the other calls
he may have gotten on duty—,
car accidents,
house raids,
traffic stops,
victims subject to robberies,
things I'll never know about—
But it was the first time
I felt comforted by him,
feeling his pulse rise,
knowing he loved me,
smiling and falling unconscious,
to wake, looking out the back window
of an ambulance, as my tears fall
simultaneously with the rain,
knowing I made a grave mistake.

FOR YOUR USE

Take a moment to reflect on the section you have just read.

What memories do you avoid remembering?
What brings about depressive feelings within you and how do you push past it?
What good can you find in your life?
Why do you persevere?

These questions are not exact. They are only to help generate thought.

Write your responses down here.

POINT OF VIEW

War and Peace

Peace does not exist
in this physical world.
You may run from where you are,
fishing in the early hours of the morning,
in the bay of the beach town
where you decided to stay,
after backpacking and wandering
country to country for two years,
and still have no peace.
Peace is internal and nothing more.
It requires meditation, reflection,
the relinquishment of your fears.

When I Go to D.C.

Push em out. Push em out. Push.

Gentrification is the erasure of culture.
One-World Uniformity
at the expense of a people
I remember dreaming
of going to Howard,
my dad would tell me
how "Hood" it was,
but hood is love, it's safety
from white people trying to overtake me.
Draining my flavah,
my spice,
straightening my curls, my naps,
influencing what I wear,
what I listen to,
not knowing the greats,
Duke Ellington,
Chuck Brown,
Rare Essence: black poetry throughout history.

When I go to D.C.,
you don't hear gogo being played
in the streets no more,
It's bike pedals, joggers frantically
breathing, lines out the Starbucks door.
It's a new Target
on the same corner
where there was a crack house.
It was "Moechella",

now it's mute D.C.!
Real estate prices
rise with eviction letters.
In my cousin's eyes,
seeing the blood of the person
they'll rob—accidentally kill—just to feel
again, knowing they're surviving,
and my aunt won't have to sleep
on the streets again.
Sadly,
my cousin will get caught,
warrants out
for his arrest,
now he's in the pen, and only
my pen will tell his story,
and others like him.
History has never cared,
and won't start
today, when I go to D.C.,
I'll stop in Northwest,
500 block of 11th Street,
where she,
my sister,
wanted to show
who's boss,
fighting against
the thing she fell
victim too: Racial Injustice, and men
trying to stick
it to the man,
will storm the nations' capitol,
breaking glass windows,

setting fire to the stairs
I once stood on
in hopes
of becoming a politician,
the dream of this dreamer
is now gone.
These insurrectionists,
living to see another day,
when my four black brothers
do not know
what the next day
will bring.

However,
tomorrow,
when I go to D.C.
I'll go to Good Hope's,
order fries,
extra old bay
mumbo sauce on the side,
and know, some
things you can't gentrify.

Black Autumn

Fall is here,
it's time for a walk.
As I lift my foot,
beginning this mile
on a cemented path,
I see multicolored leaves,
that fell from trees,
leaves,
I begin to see as myself.

These leaves are stepped on,
the groundskeepers
clear out the path,
for the privileged to walk on—
the path must remain clear,
so no one will see this Black life,
being stepped on.

The remaining leaves
on the trees
brush against each other,
protesting the mistreatment
of its fallen woe.
It's a recurring cycle,
falling, sweeping, brushing,
and when I walk this path again,
when the cycle begins,
I know fall has come,
black autumn—
only in America.

STOP!

to all the children who have been hit by cars

The red octagon
you're supposed to stop at.
Drove a quarter past,
too fast, not seeing her.
The pedals, chains, wheels
juggling in the air.
A splash across your windshield,
her eyes are open
bones making the same sound
as riding over gravel and rocks,
her eyes are still open.
Her last thought,
I just got this bike for my birthday.
her eyes are now closed.

Sir, why didn't you stop?
I can see her mother now,
cradled, crying, and cramping,
her heart is turning cold.
She'll wash and fold
her clothes every day,
Her back cracking from
the constant bending over in the dryer,
carrying a knee-length
basket to her little angel's room,
wiping the tears
falling drip-like on her shirt,

in between pulls.

Did you know little Brittney was all she had?

Sir, why didn't you stop?

Taking Time

"Take your time,"
you cannot take things that don't belong to you.
You cannot use something without
knowing how much you have.

Time is not currency.

You cannot track your last breath,
unless you're sick,

the doctor says this and that,
so, you live your life to the fullest
for the next few months
    traveling the world, living drunk, without inhibitions.
Still, that is uncertain,
doctors can be wrong because
they don't control time, it's not theirs.

"Take your time,"
is like telling a person to wait on their dreams
instead of living them, it's unrealistic,
when everything in reality exists.

"Go get it!,"
is what society should say, and they won't,
in order to maintain economic and social hierarchy,
where the bottomfeeders eat the leftovers and scraps
thrown at them or donated by those above,
however, they do not know time, and one day

time will reverse the roles, bending all that is,
    remolding the world we see into a place for everybody.

    "Take your time."
with love, this is impossible,
once you choose to commit,
you'll want to melt into their skin,
never leaving their side,
until the day you both die.

Breaks

Social media frustrates me.

It's saying happy birthday to celebrities
and not saying a word
about your friends and families'
achievements.

It's the hive mind and cancel culture
when the majority does not agree
on who the president should be,
or which community's justice takes precedence,
    from StopAsianHate, Black Americans,
    the Indigenous, to
        EndSars, TakeAKnee, MeToo, AbolishIce,
                when we all need it now.
It's the profiting off of the mistakes of those with power,
only to forget what happened next week.

It's the overuse of BLACK LIVES MATTER
when they won't matter to you next week
because now you don't see color—and even marched
once—in your world there's nothing else to confront.

This is why I take breaks from social media.
It's information overload,
like bombs hidden under seas
I'm five seconds from exploding,
rupturing the earth beneath me.

the he/art

visualize

a broken heart,

your center is vacant,

millions of sharpedged pieces,

missable due to its small size,
so vivid, there's no way to miss it
each piece, showing a memory

of pain: your first miscarriage,

of warmth: a kiss on your forehead,
as you drift asleep,

of breakthrough: finding your perfect apartment, after a year of homelessness

of power, peace,

elevation: when you started a business,
accumulating six figures,

and the memory of deterioration,
when they told you they loved another more.

as each piece falls
throughout your body,

with one piece dangling
on your ruptured aorta,
they hit your spine,
your bowels, your kidney,
pieces dissolve in your blood,
you're one with your brokenness.

having an allergic reaction,
skin begins to itch,
sensations from
every spot touched.
your mind
hears laughter,
mumbling voices,
you hear your name,
you shout, "is that you?"
then realize,
it's the television,
your longing
distorts the audio.

you sleep,
you dream,
dream of the past or maybe
a future you once hoped for—
three kids,
white picket fence,
vacations,
late nights
reminiscing about,
"when we were young".

if only we were
capable of seeing
outside of ourselves,
outside of the situation,
if only we could see
the scattered pieces
we all carry.

some of our hearts are patchwork,
a Frankenstein heart,
pitiful but hopeful.

now, visualize

all the pieces
slowly moving
back to the center.

first, your left ventricle
which holds the memories,
the laughter, their voice
every other ligament follows,
pushing yourself
closer to freedom,
closer to healing.

Les Bi Anest

I now recognize beauty,
without limitations of sexuality,
thanks to the fluidity
of my younger years.

I loved the female body,
generating much curiosity.

I aimed to please
only the woman,
it was the same
as pleasing myself.

A woman's face, eyes, lips, skin,
every detail,
the way she would walk,
how far her
smile could reach,
down to where
her waist would sit,
arousing me,
I'd long for the next time,
I'd experience a woman.

When I saw
a woman I liked,
I was in the presence
of a goddess.
If I am being honest,

being a lesbian was thrilling,
especially in secret.

I felt fire, like the
nervousness of life
in the moments where
you don't know
what will happen next.

I was living for myself,
whoever I was at that time.
Looking back,
I still do not regret
my admiration of the woman
because it helped me
love the woman
in my mirror.

I was a part of a
community lacking judgment,
which I will never forget.

Black Churches

Honoring God,
or honoring tradition?
I can come as I am spiritually,
but not physically.
Wearing dresses below the knee,
calling grown men "father",
who have never been a father to me.
Stating, "God is the head
of my life," before a sermon,
for the sake of carnal formalities.
Condemning homosexuals
but begging a woman to
let a cheater back in her home?
Stockings that must never rip,
brooches worn on the left,
because, "that's how the queen
wears it."
Knowing the queen never cared
for people of color.

This is how I was raised
and I am who I am,
but I can't help but think,
Is Yahweh pleased?

Ocean and Stars

"Heaven or Hell" they say,
but if it were up to me,
I would say "the ocean or the stars?"
To be a constellation is less pressure
than a soul forever lost in hellfire.
To be seaweed, so deep, never worrying to be plucked is
less torment than being enslaved by some devil, far worse,
than the earth I stand on.
Why can't I choose my afterlife?
Maybe then, would I live life without worry.

FOR YOUR USE

Take a moment to reflect on the section you have just read.

What about society bothers you?
What is your personal stance on any topic I have written about or any topic that comes to mind?
What discoveries have been vital to your evolving self?

These questions are not exact. They are only to help generate thought.

Write your responses down here.

religion
reMASTERed

Every Sunday

Fist in the air,
open bible
on Revelations,
preaching the end,
accepting this religious—,
maybe spiritual—,
inevitable,
amen.

Open My Heart, Lord

On bended knee,
my thoughts saying,
stop praying this prayer—
the things in me: hatred
of the sins committed against me,
seeing them and bleeding
the first boyfriend,
breaking my thumb,
as I raised it to slap him
with only his t-shirt on,
assaulting my baby cousin.

As I continue to pray,
saying—*excuse my thoughts—*
pleading, murmuring over this cross,
asking—*what did I miss?*
He didn't hit me like the last
but refused to drop the lighter,
clinging to a half dead man

Thinking—*this healing process,
making no progress,*
knowing everything I read,
from that 2700-year-old book
you left for me,
and not believing it.
Sits in my nightstand drawer,
like the ones in hotels,
motels,
collecting dust

instead of my attention,
thinking—h*ave I ever used my heart
in anything?*

Don't judge me wrong,
if I can,
I'll sleep this off, or
wake up
three times a night,
with your spirit,
always wanting to talk,
saying, "Give me your all"
I'll reply, *I'm sorry
but it's already gone,*
as my mouth backs
away from my hands.

Amen.

It Was You

Ran away at fifteen,
midnight,
spirits hugging my mind,
convincing me to leave
the house barefoot and crying,
after a thunderstorm,
the only feeling that seemed
to be mine was the
joy of not wearing socks.
Before I ran,
I let him drag me down the hall,
pass the empty dining room—,
where my parents never
thought to buy furniture—,
maybe they knew
the family would not stay long.
Reminiscing on all the traumatic things
I've seen and heard,
but cannot remember feeling
lies said to me
by principalities
of the air,
why I cared to care.

I knew my father had to love me
at one point.
I know he used to hold me
until I fell asleep,
letting my kiddrool cover
the left shoulder of his white tee.

I can envision this,
but I also see
him beating me bare,
red skinned,
later lifting as bruises.
My mother yelling at him to stop.
I knew my father had to love me
at one point.
Cheering me on
at my softball games—
I am convinced,
it was the one moment
where he did not feel shame.
If it was not the game
with that brown ball
he loves so much,
at least it was something,
and his kid would not be fat.
I can hear his cheers,
but I also hear
my mother confronting him
in secret when I was ten,
he told his friends,
"her weight is getting of hand,
I'm embarrassed."
I knew my father had to love me
at one point in my life.

These distorted memories replay,
a recap of the previous season.
It's dark out here, its late,
summer and the wind has heated thick,

But a quick, light wind
brushed against me,
from my head to my toes.
As this memory replays,
I know it was you.
You, God,
coming to comfort me.

To Hear from God

A voice heard in the mind,
asking, "What is wrong?"
A voice heard through the ears,
asking, "Can you hear me?"
whichever is unclear
lukewarm tears
fall down the side of my face.
A voice like a structure collapsing
in one instant
no seconds to spare.
Any other voice becomes debris,
as He says, "It will all be okay."
amen.

To My Abba Father

Praising; adoration fills these lips,
as I raise my arms,
hands reaching,
fingers spread open wide,
high as I can.
Obeying the you
that lives in me,
no longer breaking
dishes around me,
calling for peace when I need thee.
Enabling my faith
in you to overcome
sadness, loneliness, grief; then,
Meditating on letting go.
Eyes shut,
no sound around,
no thought,
and being content
with the feeling
of nothing
being under my control.

Amen.

FOR YOUR USE

Take a moment to reflect on the section you have just read.

What has God or your higher beings been to you?
In what ways have you felt guided by something you cannot see?
What do you believe in that you once did not believe in?

These questions are not exact. They are only to help generate thought.

Write your responses down here.

THE PURGE

so anxious

excessive worrying,
enough to fill an elephant's trunk,
then bursts out as
spurts of fatigue
raining, drenching you
wet with irritability.
muscles tense,
making it hard to move
from this mucky place,
followed by restlessness
and depression.
it will keep raining,
triggering panic attacks,
shortness of breath,
shaking, sweating,
the impending feeling
that death is near,
fears manifesting as screams,
until the only choice is
silence.

So, You Have PTSD ...

I'll never be able to enjoy foreplay without being triggered.

I'll squirm when being hugged
while my lover's arms sit at my waist.

I can't trust a hand reaching towards me,
in fear of being groped.

I'll never let anyone rub my back,
out of fear of them stepping on it.

My neck has been strangled
far more than I liked.

I'll never know the joys of physical intimacy.

Yet, I have to maintain a smile,
so I don't get sent away again.

Ever in My Heart

for my therapist

Without words, she said to me:

Growth is a journey, not a destination,
it's one you may start with hesitation.
I'll hold your hand and be your guide,
believing you can make it to the other side.

Conversation with My Therapist

Non-negotiables were the masking
of my insecurities and narcissism,
things I did, dished out,
but could never handle back.
I didn't want a smoker,
drinker, or anyone prone
to addictive behavior,
because of my own.
I found I was sensitive,
melding into the environment around me,
I can be easily swayed.
I didn't want a liar,
or a person without social morals.
But if I looked back at my mistakes,
I could see the past lovers
I made cry because of my lies.
I wanted someone accountable,
taking the blame for every argument,
constantly apologizing and under my control,
no backbone, but
they had to have goals, and a degree,
also, above six feet.
I wanted someone
to listen to everything I said
and if they missed a word,
I would hold it against them,
driving them to anger,
raising their hands to slap me.
I needed someone who
loved God because

I was lazy with prayer,
had wavering faith,
not realizing that I was the person
I did not want,
the person I hated the most.

my father in other men

you'll let me lay on your chest
and i'll think of him,

you'll bite your nails as you drive,
with all four windows down
even when it rains,
and i'll think of him

you'll buy any piece of jewelry,
especially a necklace,
and i'll think of him

i will hear you call me
by a nickname you made up,
and i'll still think of him

you may lie to me,
thinking it's better than the truth

you may be proud of me,
but have nothing,
only your words as proof

and your words,
i won't believe
because those same words
looked me in my face,
told me they would
always protect me

i constantly see
my father in other men,
the good, the bad.

sometimes i feel triggered,

other times, it's just a reminder

to pick up my phone and call him.

Her Only Supporter

Oldest daughter,
dartboard for
my mother's pain,
target for
misplaced anger.
Punching bag for
my mother's disappointments,
gray tape covering
all the rips and tears.
Ready to love her
if she lets me,
seeing her best,
like the view of God,
even when she denies it.
Truly the best child
she'll ever have,
even when I am
the only one she
claims has failed.
Her goodfornothing
baby daddy when
she needs it,
I'll feed her kids,
help with homework,
teach them their worth,
wash them, but
if there is no
child support check,
it's not enough.
The best friend

who does nothing for her,
yet, spends her last
to see her smile.
The nanny who is underpaid,
the one who tells her
my father's secrets
when her family
would rather lie
to her face—
causing more pain.
Her food stamp card,
pen used to check off
her todo list,
helping her keep
track of what
has been done.
The fork she uses
to eat her salad,
making it easier to
receive every nutrient.
The windshield wiper
when the rain
blurs her path,
the pillow she lays
her head on,
holding her neck
so it won't snap,
the only true supporter
she'll meet
in her lifetime.
The one to blame
when everyone else

around her
dies or leaves
without saying a word.
I am the river that
her traumas flow through,
it's generational.
I am her,
so, I am no one,
and anything she needs.

Or so I thought ...

When I Can't Love Myself Enough

Let these words of affirmation
caress my coco lumps,
hanging down the side of my tree,
walking out of the roots
that kept me in the ground,
strutting as if the Mona Lisa
could but brown.
Sky creatures, monkeys,
wind and sea stop to stare at me.
Gold as daffodil, white as milk,
and soft as silk,
treasures unfold
before ungrateful eyes,
of this luscious woman,
and its grease not Greece.
Blueprint, the original cup of tea,
eyes that tell nature's time,
holding the covenant
when I can't love myself enough.

Pulse

Feeling my own pulse is like
seeing my life flash before your eyes.
From exiting the womb and hearing my first cry
to reliving the torment of bullying,
wishing I would have stood up sooner.
From seeing my mother's brown skin
turn blue and purple,
to now, what I see as growing
amethysts and pansies
because all it did
was make her bloom.
From riding down a hill,
caterpillars in my bike pouch,
taking them out,
electric bites
stimulating my hand.
To the joy of delivering puppies,
only to find one has already died.
From the relief of being
at my high school graduation,
when two weeks prior,
keen on no afterlife,
I felt brave enough to take my life.
To this day where I lay down,
staring into the constellations
my nightlight exhibits,
longing to sync
my breath with my pulse,
healing and moving
to one of Mercury's moons.

Metamorphosis

As a child,
I would pick caterpillars
off the ground,
place them in my blue
bike's pouch, ride down
the hill on my street,
full of 1980s homes,
screaming to the top
of my lungs,

*when i take these
caterpillars out,
they will be butterflies,*

ignorant to how
metamorphosis actually worked.

Ironically, my bike
was covered in butterflies.

Upon stopping
at the bottom of the hill,
I would reach
inside my pouch
to take them out,
and they would bite me.
You see caterpillars
have a fear of leaving the ground, they cling to it,
until they are ready
to wiggle up a tree,

build a chrysalis
around their body
to protect it,
and prepare themselves to be a butterfly that will cling
to the sky,
flying endlessly in it,
only landing
to give its wings a rest.

Caterpillars are
the closest thing
in nature to humans.
Excuse me, they are
the closest thing
to the healing process
and the result.
We cling to our past trauma—
the ground—
climbing the tree
is acknowledgement of our pain,
saying yes to the process.
The chrysalis is the application,
and the butterfly
is what we become
once we allow ourselves
freedom to go
anywhere or move
in any way we please.

Moon Phases

Healing is a process,
like the phasing of the moon.
It's new when you first begin,
growing into a waxing crescent
as you choose
which battle to overcome—
maybe loving the skin you are in—
maybe the person
you chose to forgive.
Then you're near full like
the waxing gibbous,
and when you're at
the moment of fullness
you experience an awakening,
essentially your spirit is growing.
As it grows,
a trauma resurfaces,
bringing you down
to a waning gibbous.
Finally, a waning crescent, all
to begin this cycle again.
Healing is lifelong,
like the phasing of the moon.

Soul Saver

Therapy saves your soul from growing darker,
to an equivalence of numbness,
to the point where help falls on deaf ears,
to where you choose not to eat—
only smoke and drink—
to when you run away,
living off the essence of others,
to the moment you hurt
someone else in a way
you can never take back.
Therapy saves your soul
from eternal darkness,
allowing you to talk
through everything,
assigning emotions,
practicing wholesome habits—
like looking in the mirror,
telling your skin it is gorgeous—
saying how you feel
misunderstood instead
of shouting, "i hate you!"
 It's about journaling,
extinction of gaslighting,
aiming to reach a pinnacle
discovering your identity,
recognizing purpose,
living for yourself.
Therapy saved my soul
from being taken,
let it save yours too.

FOR YOUR USE

Take a moment to reflect on the section you have just read.

Do you think therapy may be beneficial to you?
If you are already in therapy, what lessons have you learned that you may have forgotten?
What does healing feel like to you?
What are you denying or pushing deep down within your subconscious?

These questions are not exact. They are only to help generate thought.

Write your responses down here.

THE F WORD

My Kobe

recollection of a dream about my father

Celebrating in a big arena,
don't worry,
this time it's no subpoenas
with judges speaking
of child support.
You lived a life,
left a legacy
as big as Kobe's,
and that's how you
came to me
in a dream,
as one of your idols.
Your arm,
with your mamba tattoo,
wrapped around my shoulder
taking a selfie
elated that I finally
met somebody famous.

How to Move on When They Cut Your Legs

You get prosthetics,
or a wheel chair,
maybe wake one day
with the power of limb
regeneration, like a titan
in that one anime.

You may never
run the same, but
mobility is still possible,
and though they
cut my legs,
I am not defeated,
and neither are you.

Forgiving Me

As I hold the hand
of my elevenyearold self
before boarding this train,
adamant on never letting go,
I think back to all the moments
where I abandoned my soul.

Letting my body travel
station to station,
meeting new people,
making carnal connections,
learning new things,
thinking I was growing,
but I was still eleven,
I never truly aged

I didn't know forgiveness,
I refused to recognize trauma,
until I came back to the station,
to pick up my adolescent soul.

I told her I was sorry
for ignoring the calls from within,
she told me it was okay,
and that she knew I'd return.
This station was home,
a place everyone comes back to.

FOR YOUR USE

Take a moment to reflect on the section you have just read.

I know forgiveness is hard, but it is possible.
Is there anything you need to forgive?

Write your response down here.

The Benediction

The Enslaved and the Master

Slave to my fear
of the things behind me,
trying to greet me
when I'm in the heat.
Master of overcoming,
with the turbulence of a river
that's deep.
However, I am still a
slave too, that needle
sticking me with
mosquitolike bite anxiety,
in this bayou,
on this boat,
you see my crippling sweats.
Slave too, those one dollar
sheets from 7-11
that were killing me but,
somehow, I beat.
Slave too, that last quarter
of Hennessey with
a line of coke,
at this point,
I was losing hope.
Slave too, my parents
kicking me out,
sleeping in my car,
no job, no money,
it was a drought.
But I am the master
of my former,

which He brought me out.

I have a slave and master mentality,
that's my double consciousness,
that's Moses and Pharaoh,
that's Samson and Delilah,
that's Jesus and the Jews,
that's David and Goliath,
it's Saul versus Paul,
it's hatred overpowering fear
or fears holding you back from freedom,
but then it's God and the devil inside
and in the long ride,
God always gets the last stride.
So, I'll rise like a resurrection
because one day
I'll just be the master,
never wavering in
the midst of these roaring tides.

From My Flesh to My Spirit

For years I chose
to not embrace
things innate to me,
all along
you did it with
no complaints,
helping me love
the ripples in my back,
the mole on my neck,
the smile I hid away,
the sight of which my lover implores,
hair I concealed with fakes,
forgetting my scalp,
watching it fall out.
The voice I had no control over
now producing melodies,
colleagues, friends,
strangers beg to hear.
The mind that consumes me,
leading me to write a book,
take charge of our dreams.
The arms that are truly wings,
you told me I could be free,
now look at me,
cherishing my beauty,
that you longed for at first sight.

If I Could Change Anything, It Would Be Me ...

not the world,
cause the world
can't make me free.

I guess I'd start
with my state of mind
instead of trying
to conquer world peace,
lovin' on every valley
encompassing my temple,
positive affirmations,
I believe they call it.

The world could
spit me out its mouth
and I'd still live,
with no need
for a respirator.

Bringing some of that love
I pushed outward,
pulling it back in,
letting it find
its way back
to where it belonged.

Lemons to Lemonade, Lemon Cake, Lemon Pie

Life gave me lemons
unwarranted,
teaching lessons,
pain,
the cost of pleasure

Lemonade,
something sweet
that washed down
the bitter residue

Lemon Cake,
its icing,
amplifying the taste
of life's plain batter

Lemon Pie,
not just a slice,
but the whole thing

I held my brittle crust
until its promises
were fulfilled

Now, I'll reap the benefits
of lemons to lemonade,
lemon cake, lemon pie,
this is my life.

Virgo

You evolve
with the times,
Mother Nature
personified,
protecting life
in the background,
a guardian angel,
limitless faith
even when stress hits.
Spirits run amuck
telling you lies,
that you're not
good enough,
that nothing is
good enough,
you didn't make
summer warm enough,
your tulips
aren't colorful enough.
The fall leaves
didn't capture
anyone's eyes,
even in winter,
when they try
to take your last breath,
you'll overcome
because you are Virgo.
Let people
embrace you,
bathing in

your waters,
laying naked
in your forests,
walking
hidden paths,
and climbing mountains.
Let them see the world
from your view
and now they won't
destroy you.

Sanctuary

Thankful for the midnights
when I walked through
your tawny double doors.
Dimmed lights,
taper candles lit,
corduroy chairs
spread at the altar,
and pillows for the knees
that kneeled for hours.
I carried a spiral notebook
and pen, with intentions to
write down all I wanted
to pray for after meditation,
after I attended my therapy
session for the month.
You were the one place
where my religion
danced with my spirituality,
protecting me from
negative energy that would
persuade my emotions
to think falsely
on what physical abominations
happened to me as a child,
on forgiveness and if
it was ever attainable,
on self-identity,
working to recognize
the person I see in the mirror.
I was covered in divine essence,

achieving spiritual excellence,
recognizing my perspective,
healing in an instant,
realizing that I must
always come back to you,
for myself and others
that will need you.

FOR YOUR USE

Take a moment to reflect on the section you have just read.

What have you discovered after reading this entire collection?
What do you want to take with you?
What stories do you carry that have not been told?

These questions are not exact. They are only to help generate thought.

Write your responses down here.

ACKNOWLEDGEMENTS

When setting out on a long journey you have never embarked on before, you never know how much work it will take to reach your final destination. I have discovered along my journey of writing *Sanctuary,* that publishing a book takes a village, and I am so grateful for all of the support. Fulfilling this dream would not have been possible without you.

Thank you first and foremost to my family for supporting me through every step of the way, always ...

Thank you to those that donated and pre-ordered:

The Herron Family, Ella Vaught-Gardner, Jazmyne Terry, Erica Akins, Lauren Krasnodembski, Camille Briscoe, Glenn Martin, Reilly Vore, True Devine, Shakila Rana, Renee Lewis, Talaysha Hooper-Martin, Destini Williams, Eric Koester, Sabrina Crusoe, Chanel Swinton, Lori Johnson, Kathy Gibbs, Dionne Regis, Anna Pedro-Jackson, Claire Lewinski, Gillaila Thomas, Miriam Hester, Jeric Lewis, Rasheed Sparks, Lafon Hamilton, Pedro Rancier, Michael Fermaint, Zakiyyah Mahasin, Joe Lawston, Tahja Norman, Pamela Ingram,

Niharika Shah, Chermine Trotman, Danielle Miles, Brittnee Ross, Dana Wiggins, Micah Bennett, Marqui Williams, Tanika Mance, Lamon Hamilton Sr., Tiffany Whaley, Mariama Patterson D'uana Coley, Tanica Bagmon, Marissa Savory, Chanda Everhart, Mary Thomas, Leetoya Robinson, Myles Jackson, Kecia Burnett, Mike Picchiello, Paris Anthony, Deasia Revels, Evelyn Sexton-Wiggins, Kennedy Ford, Marie Samuel, Michael Price, Zhuri Winfree, Jada Vaught, LaVeetra Jenkins, Heddrick Mcbride, Cassidy Martin, Stephanie Cole, Natacha Vainqueur, Karla Pickett, Verna Pickett, Dennis Countiss, Mariah Ruth, Isaiah Sauls, Thecla Brown, Jackson Long, Lydia Ford, Tawanda Davis, Tamara Gordon, Monique Johnson, Katy Lopez, Chiemeka Obi, Sade Killette, Leslie Fluker, Tanja Davis-Cochran, Stephan Warner, Christine Simmons, Christopher Solano.

www.ingramcontent.com/pod-product-compliance
Lightning Source LLC
LaVergne TN
LVHW011837060526
838200LV00053B/4070